ALSO BY MAISIE SPARKS

151 Things God Can't Do

HOLY SHAKESPEARE!

101 Scriptures That Appear in Shakespeare's Plays, Poems, and Sonnets

MAISIE SPARKS

NEW YORK | BOSTON | NASHVILLE

FaithWords
Hachette Book Group
1290 Avenue of the Americas, New York, NY 10104
faithwords.com
twitter.com/faithwords

First Edition: October 2016

FaithWords is a division of Hachette Book Group, Inc. The FaithWords
name and logo are trademarks of Hachette Book Group, Inc.

The publisher is not responsible for websites (or their content) that are not
owned by the publisher.

The Hachette Speakers Bureau provides a wide range of authors for
speaking events. To find out more, go to www.hachettespeakersbureau.com
or call (866) 376-6591.

ISBNs: 978-1-4555-7042-3 (hardcover), 978-1-4555-7041-6 (ebook)

Printed in the United States of America

WOR

10   9   8   7   6   5   4   3   2   1

ACKNOWLEDGMENTS

Writing is a solitary art, but every writer benefits from family, friends, and supporters who provide the prayer, encouragement, and advice needed to stay the course so that blank computer screens can be filled with words worth reading. My deepest gratitude to my family for gracing me with countless solitary hours to write.

Thanks to Mark Boone, editor and encourager, who helps me to think through what I really want to say, and to James Marc Pressley and the Shakespeare Resource Center for insights into Shakespeare and for coming up with the title for this book. Finally, thanks to Adrienne Ingram, my editor at Hachette Book Group, and Rolf Zettersten, publisher, for giving me the opportunity to write this book and discover again that our greatest work is always based on God's Word.

PLAYS ON GOD'S WORD

Four hundred years after his death, William Shakespeare is still considered the greatest playwright of all time. Could that be because he knew intimately the Greatest Book of all the ages? His plays, poems, and sonnets are filled with scriptural allusions and biblical imagery that, if you're not discerning, might slip right by you.

For years they certainly passed me by. Not until recently did I see the similarities between Shakespeare's writings and the Holy Writ. I might have received a much better grade in my English Lit class had I only noticed that his works referenced many of the Bible stories and teachings that I was learning in Sunday school.

Unlike me, however, Shakespeare's sixteenth-century audiences understood the biblical allusions that the Great Bard made, for he lived in what's been called a biblical culture and era. People grew up learning to read by reading the Bible. Shoppers on the London Bridge might stop to listen to traveling actors who were performing a play based on a Bible story. Churches used dramatizations extensively to teach and enact the Word of God. Along with writing out the alphabet, schoolchildren might print a verse or two from the Geneva Bible—the version that you'll read on these pages. Contemporaries of Shakespeare felt right at home with the Bible, as it was a staple read in homes. With Scripture permeating the culture, it's easy to see how holy sentiments appeared on paper when Shakespeare sat down to write.

What's been fascinating to me in rereading Shakespeare is how copious his use of Scripture is this time around. The Bible is right there…hidden in plain sight. Many lovers of Shakespeare have known this fact for centuries, but over the years the study of both Shakespeare and the Bible has waned in homes, schools, and churches.

That's why I've written *Holy Shakespeare!* It's intended to awaken your curiosity for more of Shakespeare's timeless works and, at the same time, the Great Creator's Eternal Word. *Holy Shakespeare!* is not an exhaustive listing of every reference to Scripture that Shakespeare ever made; it's an invitation to taste and see how masterfully creative he was at weaving the Word seamlessly into his works. I've paired lines from Shakespeare with passages from the Bible and interspersed some facts about Shakespeare for you to reflect on as you read the pairings. It's my desire that reading *Holy Shakespeare!* will instill in you a greater appreciation of Shakespeare and a heightened awareness of God's Word as reflected in his works.

So, turn the page, savor Shakespeare anew, and reflect on God's Word. Along the way, I pray that you will gain strength in the recognition of its enduring power.

HOLY SHAKESPEARE!

1. worthy praise

Do's not the Stone rebuke me,
For being more Stone then it?

THE WINTER'S TALE, ACT V, SCENE 3

Then some of the Pharisees of the company said unto him, Master, rebuke thy disciples. But he answered, and said unto them, I tell you, that if these should hold their peace, the stones would cry.

LUKE 19:39–40

2. the perfect sacrifice

> With that dread King that took our state
>   upon Him
> To free us from his Father's wrathful curse.

KING HENRY VI PART II, ACT III, SCENE 2

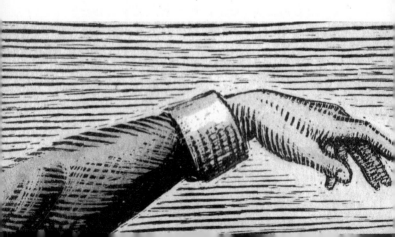

For he hath made him to be sin for us, which knew no sin, that we should be made the righteousness of God in him.

II CORINTHIANS 5:21

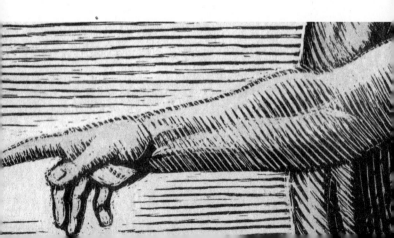

3. accountability

> Though some of you, with Pilate, wash your
>   hands,
> Shewing an outward pitie: yet you Pilates
> Have here deliver'd me to my sowre crosse,
> And Water cannot wash away your sinne.
>
> KING RICHARD II, ACT IV, SCENE 1

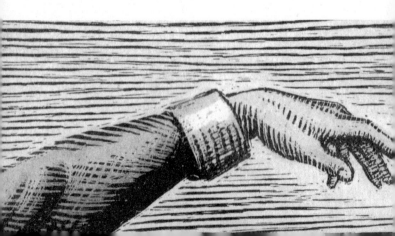

When Pilate saw that he availed nothing, but that more tumult was made, he took water and washed his hands before the multitude, saying, I am innocent of the blood of this just man: look you to it.

MATTHEW 27:24

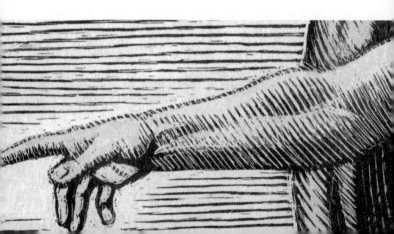

4. Christ, the example

A virtuous and Christian-like conclusion,
To pray for them that have done scathe to us.

KING RICHARD III, ACT I, SCENE 3

But I say unto you which hear, love your enemies:
do well to them which hate you. Bless them that
curse you, and pray for them which hurt you.

LUKE 6:27–28

5. Jesus, the ransom

…the world's ransome, blessed Mary's Sonne.

KING RICHARD II, ACT II, SCENE 1

*Even as the Son of man came not to be served,
but to serve, and to give his life for the ransom of
many.*

MATTHEW 20:28

The preamble to William Shakespeare's will includes these words: "I commend my soul into the hands of God my Creator, hoping and assuredly believing through the only merits of Jesus Christ my Saviour to be made partaker of life everlasting."

6. worthy leaders

I have seen the dumb men throng to see him,
   and
The blind to hear him speak….

CORIOLANUS, ACT II, SCENE 1

And, great multitudes came unto him, having with them, halt, blind, dumb, maimed and many others, and cast them down at Jesus' feet, and he healed them.

MATTHEW 15:30

7. personal worth

...there is special providence in the fall of a
sparrow.

HAMLET, PRINCE OF DENMARK, ACT V, SCENE 2

*Are not two sparrows sold for a farthing, and one
of them shall not fall on the ground without your
Father? Yea, and all the hairs of your head are
numbered. Fear ye not therefore, ye are of more
value than many sparrows.*

MATTHEW 10:29–31

8. division and destruction

> Oh! If you reare this House against this
>   House
> It will the woefullest division prove,
> That ever fell upon this cursed Earth.

KING RICHARD II, ACT V, SCENE 2

But Jesus knew their thoughts, and said to them,
Every kingdom divided against itself, shall be
brought to naught: and every city or house,
divided against itself shall not stand.

MATTHEW 12:25

9. false affection

To say the truth, so Judas kist his master,
And cried all haile! when as he meant all
   harme.

KING HENRY VI PART III, ACT V, SCENE 7

*And Jesus said unto him, Judas, betrayest thou
the Son of man with a kiss?*

LUKE 22:48

10. the devil's truth, deception

The devil can cite Scripture for his purpose.
An evil soul producing holy witness
Is like a villain with a smiling cheek,
A goodly apple rotten at the heart.
O, what a goodly outside falsehood hath!

THE MERCHANT OF VENICE, ACT I, SCENE 3

Then the devil took him up into the Holy City, and set him on a pinnacle of the Temple, And said unto him, If thou be the Son of God, cast thyself down: for it is written, that he will give his Angels charge over thee, and with their hands they shall lift thee up, lest at any time you shouldest dash thy foot against a stone. Jesus said unto him, It is written again, Thou shalt not tempt the Lord thy God.

MATTHEW 4:5–7

II. clarity

…by yea, and no, I doe.

THE MERRY WIVES OF WINDSOR, ACT I, SCENE 1

But let your communication be Yea, yea: Nay,
nay. For whatsoever is more than these, cometh
of evil.

MATTHEW 5:37

The Geneva translation of the Bible was the first English translation to add numbered verses to the chapters to make finding passages easier.

12. impartiality

The quality of mercy is not strain'd.
It droppeth as the gentle raine from heaven
Upon the place beneath.

THE MERCHANT OF VENICE, ACT IV, SCENE 1

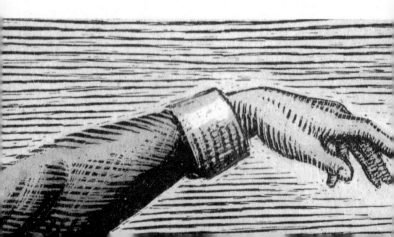

…For he maketh his sun to arise on the evil, and
the good, and sendeth rain on the just, and unjust.

MATTHEW 5:45

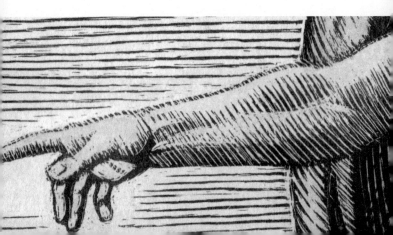

13. justice tempered with mercy

And earthly power doth then show likest God's
When mercy seasons justice.

THE MERCHANT OF VENICE, ACT IV, SCENE 1

Then the Scribes, and the Pharisees brought unto
him a woman, taken in adultery, and set her

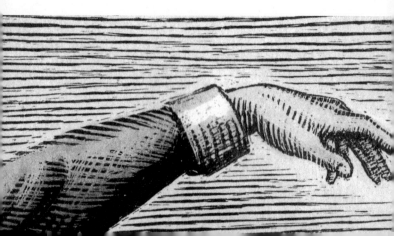

in the midst, And said unto him, Master, this woman was taken in adultery, in the very act. Now Moses in the Law commanded us, that such should be stoned: what sayest thou therefore? And this they said to tempt him, that they might have, whereof to accuse him. But Jesus stooped down, and with his finger wrote on the ground. And while they continued asking him, he lifted himself up, and said unto them, Let him that is among you without sin, cast the first stone at her.

JOHN 8:3–7

14. evil desires

All offences, my Lord, come from the heart.

KING HENRY V, ACT IV, SCENE 8

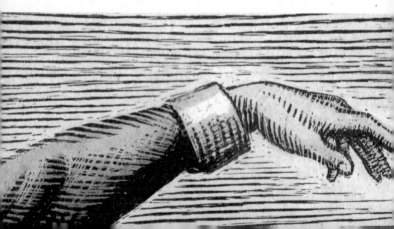

Then he said, That which cometh out of man, that defileth man. For from within, even out of the heart of men, proceed evil thoughts, adulteries, fornications, murders, Thefts, covetousness, wickedness, deceit, uncleanness, a wicked eye, backbiting, pride, foolishness. All these evil things come from within, and defile a man.

MARK 7:20–23

15. fast and disastrous

> If it were done when 'tis done, then 'twere
>   well
> It were done quickly.

THE TRAGEDY OF MACBETH ACT I, SCENE 7

*And after the sop, Satan entered into him. Then
said Jesus unto him, That thou doest, do quickly.*

JOHN 13:27

16. sin's paycheck

All Friends shall taste the wages of their
    vertue, and all Foes
The cup of their deservings: O see, see.

KING LEAR, ACT V, SCENE 3

For the wages of sin is death: but the gift of God is
eternal life through Jesus Christ our Lord.

ROMANS 6:23

17. fallen star

Ah! Richard, with the eyes of heavie mind,
I see thy Glory like a shooting Starre.
Fall to the base Earth from the Firmament.

KING RICHARD II, ACT II, SCENE 4

And he said unto them, I saw Satan, like lightning,
fall down from heaven.

LUKE 10:18

18. jealousy

Which blood, like sacrificing Abel's, cries,
even from the tongueless caverns of the earth,
to me for justice and rough chastisement;
And, by the glorious worth of my descent,
this arm shall do it, or this life be spent.

KING RICHARD II, ACT I, SCENE 1

Again he said, What hast thou done? the voice of
thy brother's blood crieth unto me, from the earth.

GENESIS 4:10

The Bible story that appears most often in Shakespeare's writings is the story of Cain and Abel.

19. selfish demands

> …what prodigall portion have I spent, that I
> should come to such penury?

AS YOU LIKE IT, ACT I, SCENE 1

And the younger of them said to his father, Father,
give me the portion of the goods that falleth to me.
So he divided unto them his substance.

LUKE 15:12

20. pride's finale

Cromwel, I charge thee, fling away Ambition,
By that sinne fell the Angels: how can man
   then
(the image of his Maker) hope to win by it?

KING HENRY VIII, ACT III, SCENE 2

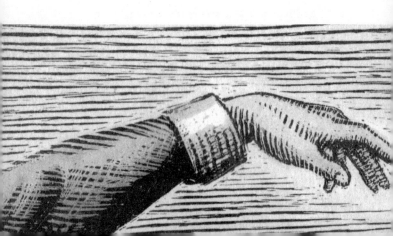

How art thou fallen from heaven, O Lucifer, son of the morning? And cut down to the ground, which didst cast lots upon the nations? Yet thou saidest in thine heart, I will ascend into heaven, and exalt my throne above beside the stars of God: I will sit also upon the mount of the congregation in the sides of the north. I will ascend above the height of the clouds, and I will be like the most high. But thou shalt be brought down to the grave, to the sides of the pit.

ISAIAH 14:12–15

21. bankrupted

Shall I keepe your hogs, and eat huskes with
  them?

AS YOU LIKE IT, ACT 1, SCENE 1

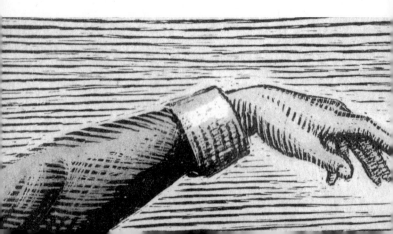

Now when he had spent all, there arose a great dearth throughout that land, and he began to be in necessity. Then he went and clave to a citizen of that country, and he sent him to his farm, to feed swine. And he would fain have filled his belly with the husks that the swine ate: but no man gave them him.

LUKE 15:14–16

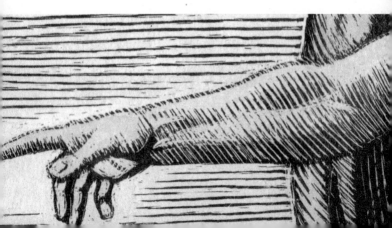

22. deceivers

And thus I clothe my naked villainy
With odd old ends stol'n forth of holy writ,
And seem a saint when most I play the devil.

KING RICHARD III, ACT I, SCENE 3

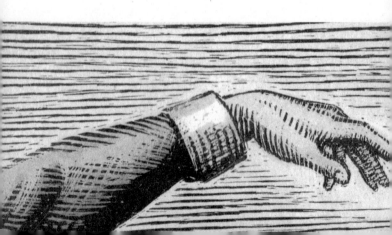

Beware of false prophets, which come to you in sheep's clothing, but inwardly they are ravening wolves.

MATTHEW 7:15

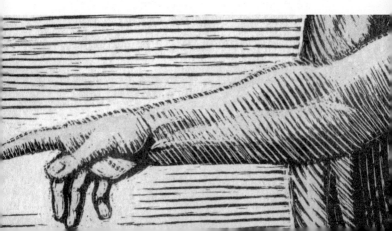

23. haunting guilt

Whence is that knocking?
How is't with me, when every noise appals me?

THE TRAGEDY OF MACBETH, ACT II, SCENE 2

And upon them that are left of you, I will send even a faintness into their hearts in the land of their enemies, and the sound of a leaf shaken shall chase them, and they shall flee as fleeing from a sword, and they shall fall, no man pursuing them.

LEVITICUS 26:36

To use the idioms "all that glitters is not gold," "shame the devil by telling the truth," "last, not least," "wild-goose chase," "brave new world," "it's Greek to me," "neither rhyme nor reason," "kill with kindness," "in a pickle," "a laughingstock," or "Knock, knock! Who's there?" is to quote Shakespeare.

24. denial

Few love to hear the sins they love to act.

PERICLES, PRINCE OF TYRE, ACT I, SCENE 1

*And this is the condemnation, that light is come
into the world, and men loved darkness rather
than light, because their deeds were evil.*

JOHN 3:19

25. fatal pride

Would he not stumble? Would he not fall
   downe,
(Since pride must have a fall), and breake the
   necke
Of that proud man, that did usurp his backe?

KING RICHARD II, ACT V, SCENE 4

*Before destruction the heart of a man is haughty,
and before glory goeth lowliness.*

PROVERBS 18:12

26. deception

And oftentimes, to win us to our harm,
The instruments of darkness tell us truths.

THE TRAGEDY OF MACBETH, ACT I, SCENE 3

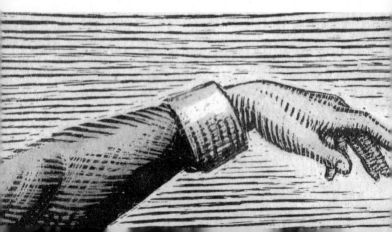

Then the serpent said to the woman, Ye shall not die at all, But God doth know, that when ye shall eat thereof, your eyes shall be opened, and ye shall be as gods, knowing good and evil.

GENESIS 3:4–5

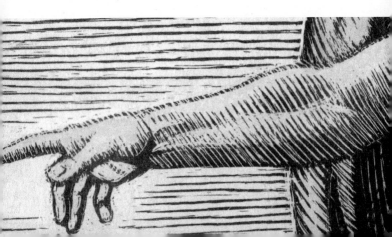

27. being brought low

I am no great Nebuchadnezzar, Sir; I have not
much skill in grass.

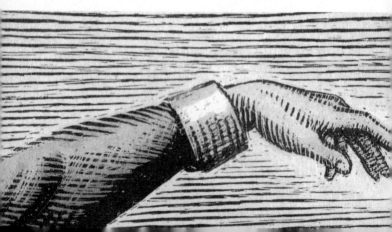

The very same hour was this thing fulfilled upon Nebuchadnezzar, and he was driven from men, and did eat grass as the oxen, and his body was wet with the dew of heaven, till his hairs were grown as eagles' feathers, and his nails like birds' claws.

DANIEL 4:33

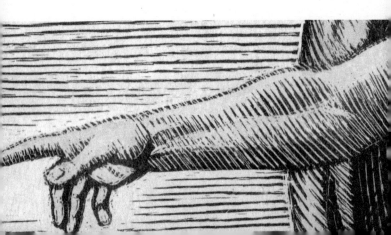

28. reckoning day

But in these cases we still have judgement
    here, that we but teach
Bloody instructions, which, being taught
    return
To plague the inventor.

THE TRAGEDY OF MACBETH, ACT I, SCENE 7

*Be not deceived: God is not mocked: for
whatsoever a man soweth, that shall he also reap.*

GALATIANS 6:7

Linking a biblical person to a fictional character represents the use of allusion, the literary device employed by writers to provide insight into the character. In *The Tragedy of Macbeth*, the character Macbeth is likened to the God-forsaken King Saul, who also consulted with witches instead of the omniscient God.

29. hypocrisy

And some that smile have in their hearts, I
   fear,
Millions of mischiefs.

JULIUS CAESAR, ACT IV, SCENE 1

*Draw me not away with the wicked, and with the
workers of iniquity: which speak friendly to their
neighbors, when malice is in their hearts.*

PSALM 28:3

30. ill-gotten gain

Nought's had, all's spent,
Where our desire is got without content.

THE TRAGEDY OF MACBETH, ACT III, SCENE 2

Then he gave them their desire: but he sent leanness into their soul.

PSALM 106:15

31. fiery furnace

> Be advis'd;
> Heat not a furnace for your foe so hot
> That it do sindge your selfe.

KING HENRY VIII, ACT I, SCENE 1

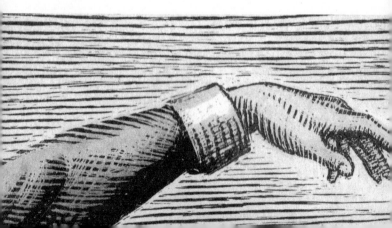

Therefore, because the king's commandment was straight, that the furnace should be exceeding hot, the flame of the fire slew those men that brought forth Shadrach, Meshach and Abednego.

DANIEL 3:22

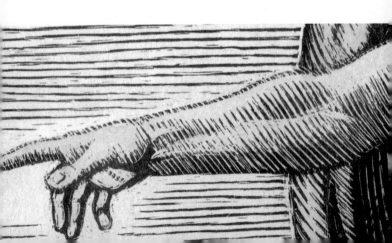

32. repentance

O Lord have mercy on me, wofull man!

KING HENRY VI PART I, ACT I, SCENE 4

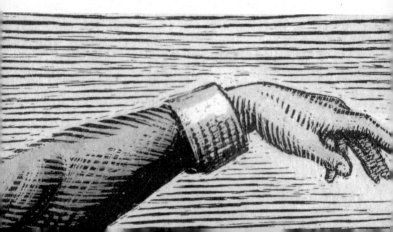

Have mercy upon me, O God, according to thy loving kindness: according to the multitude of thy compassions put away mine iniquities.

PSALM 51:1

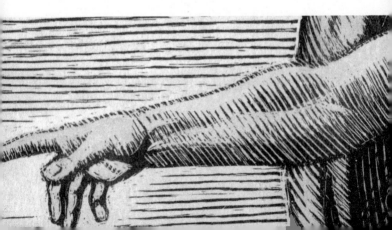

33. hoarding

If thou art rich, thou'rt poor;
for like an ass whose back with ingots bows,
Thou bear'st thy heavy riches but a journey,
And Death unloads thee.

MEASURE FOR MEASURE, ACT III, SCENE 1

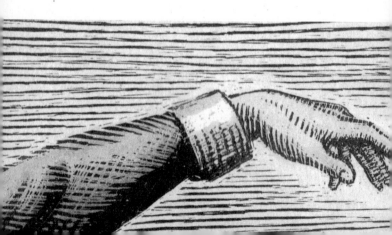

And I will say to my soul, Soul, thou hast much goods laid up for many years: live at ease, eat, drink, and take thy pastime. But God said unto him, O fool, this night will they fetch away thy soul from thee: then whose shall those things be which thou hast provided?

LUKE 12:19–20

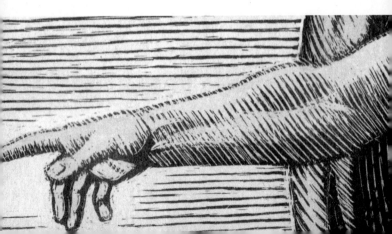

The London Bridge that William Shakespeare would have walked across looked more like a street than a bridge because it was lined with homes and shops.

34. vengeance

Yea, yea, my lord; I'll yield him thee asleep,
Where thou may'st knock a nail into his head.

THE TEMPEST, ACT III, SCENE 2

Then Jael Heber's wife took a nail of the tent, and took an hammer in her hand, and went softly unto him, and smote the nail into his temples, and fastened it into the ground, (for he was fast asleep and weary) and so he died.

JUDGES 4:21

35. boomerang

O God, what mischiefes work the wicked
   ones?
Heaping confusion on their owne heads
   thereby!

KING HENRY VI PART II, ACT II, SCENE 1

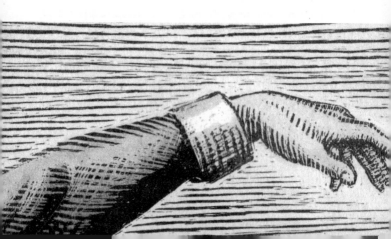

*His mischief shall return upon his own head, and
his cruelty shall fall upon his own pate.*

PSALM 7:16

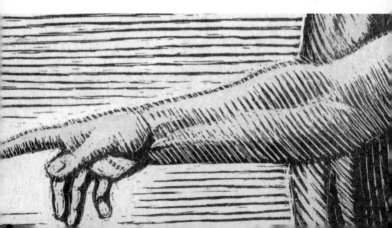

36. regretful words

To keep that oath, were more impiety
Than Jephthah's when he sacrific'd his daughter.

KING HENRY VI PART III, ACT V, SCENE 1

*And Jephthah vowed a vow unto the Lord, and
said, If thou shalt deliver the children of Ammon
into mine hands, Then that thing that cometh out*

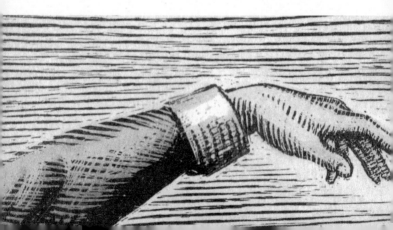

of the doors of mine house to meet me, when I come home in peace from the children of Ammon, shall be the Lord's, and I will offer it for a burnt offering.... Now when Jephthah came to Mizpeh unto his house, behold, his daughter came out to meet him with timbrels and dances, which was his only child: he had none other son, nor daughter. And when he saw her, he rent his clothes, and said, Alas my daughter, thou hast brought me low, and art of them that trouble me: for I have opened my mouth unto the Lord, and cannot go back.

JUDGES 11:30–31, 34–35

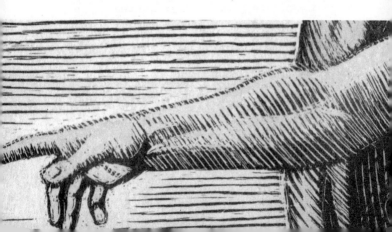

37. the wages of sin

The time shall come that foul sin, gathering
   head,
shall break into corruption....

KING HENRY IV PART II, ACT III, SCENE 1

*Then when lust hath conceived, it bringeth forth
sin, and sin when it is finished, bringeth forth
death.*

JAMES 1:15

38. paranoia

Suspicion always haunts the guilty mind;
The thief doth fear each bush an officer.

KING HENRY VI PART III, ACT V, SCENE 6

*But the wicked are like the raging sea that cannot
rest, whose waters cast up mire and dirt. There is
no peace, saith my God, to the wicked.*

ISAIAH 57:20–21

39. revenge

Let heaven revenge: for I may never lift
An angry arme against his Minister.

KING RICHARD II, ACT I, SCENE 2

And he said unto his men, The Lord keep me from doing that thing unto my master the Lord's anointed, to lay mine hand upon him: for he is the anointed of the Lord. So David overcame his servants with these words, and suffered them not to arise against Saul: so Saul rose up out of the cave and went away.

I SAMUEL 24:7–8

Religious upheaval was common during the sixteenth and seventeenth centuries. Kings and queens were constantly re-establishing England's religious allegiance based on personal interests, political alliances, or spiritual convictions. Being on the wrong side of a monarch's religious beliefs could result in death.

40. hidden sins

Who covers faults, at last with shame derides:

KING LEAR, ACT I, SCENE 1

He that hideth his sins, shall not prosper: but he that confesseth, and forsaketh them, shall have mercy.

PROVERBS 28:13

41. deadly words

…'Tis slander,
Whose edge is sharper than the sword, whose
tongue
Outvenoms all the worms of Nile….

CYMBELINE, ACT III, SCENE 4

But the tongue can no man tame. It is an unruly
evil, full of deadly poison.

JAMES 3:8

42. vanity

What win I, if I gain the thing I seek?
A dream, a breath, a froth of fleeting joy.
Who buys a minute's mirth to wail a week?
Or sells eternity to get a toy?

THE RAPE OF LUCRECE

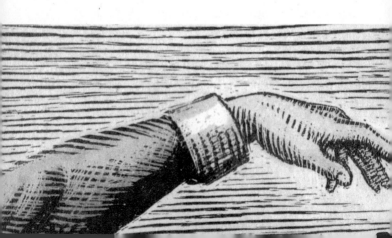

And whatsoever mine eyes desired, I withheld it
not from them: I withdrew not mine heart from
any joy: for mine heart rejoiced in all my labor:
and this was my portion of all my travail. Then
I looked on all my works that mine hands had
wrought, and on the travail that I had labored to
do: and behold, all is vanity and vexation of the
spirit: and there is no profit under the sun.

ECCLESIASTES 2:10–11

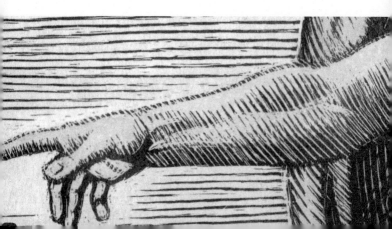

43. personal integrity

This above all,—to thine own self be true;
And it must follow, as the night the day,
Thou canst not then be false to any man.

HAMLET, PRINCE OF DENMARK ACT I, SCENE 3

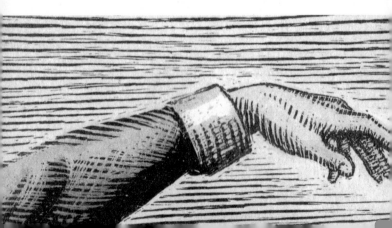

But Peter and John answered unto them, and said, Whether it be right in the sight of God, to obey you rather than God, judge ye. For we cannot but speak the things which we have seen and heard.

ACTS 4:19–20

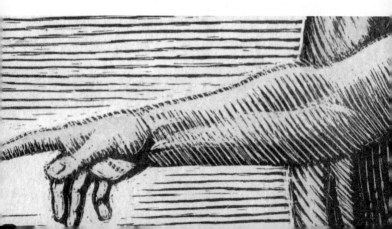

Despite opposition from religious leaders in England and Rome, William Tyndale translated and published the New Testament into a clear English prose in 1526. Tyndale's clear writing style provided much of the foundation for the Geneva Bible, which Shakespeare more than likely read as a child.

44. evil appetites

Pity the world, or else this glutton be,
To eat the world's due, by the grave and thee.

SONNET 1

Whose end is damnation, whose God is their belly, and whose glory is to their shame, which mind earthly things.

PHILIPPIANS 3:19

45. inner turmoil

Men at some time are masters of their fates:
The fault, dear Brutus, is not in our stars,
But in ourselves, that we are underlings.

THE TRAGEDY OF JULIUS CAESAR, ACT I, SCENE 2

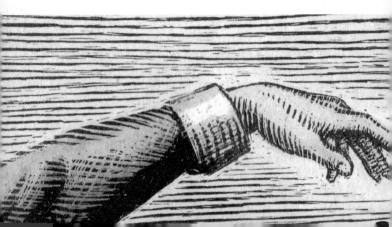

From whence are wars and contentions among you? are they not hence, even of your lusts, that fight in your members? Ye lust, and have not: ye envy, and have indignation, and cannot obtain: ye fight and war, and get nothing, because ye ask not. Ye ask, and receive not because ye ask amiss, that ye might consume it on your lusts.

JAMES 4:1–3

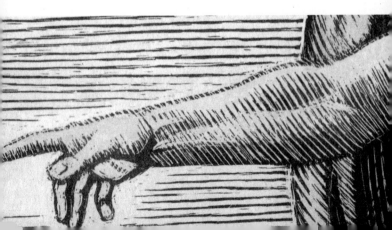

46. appearances

...from the crown of his head to the sole of
his foot he is all mirth....

MUCH ADO ABOUT NOTHING, ACT III, SCENE 2

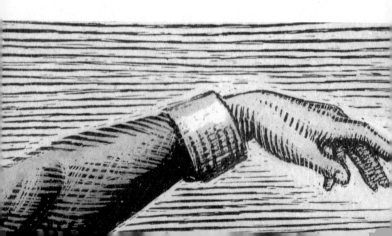

Now in all Israel there was none to be so much praised for beauty as Absalom: from the sole of his foot even to the top of his head there was no blemish in him.

II SAMUEL 14:25

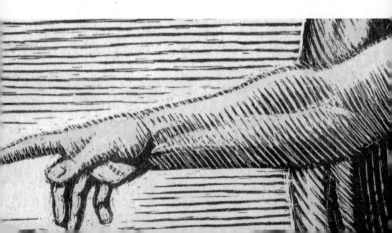

47. grief

O Grandsire, Grandsire: even with all my
   heart
Would I were Dead so you did Live againe.

TITUS ANDRONICUS, ACT V, SCENE 3

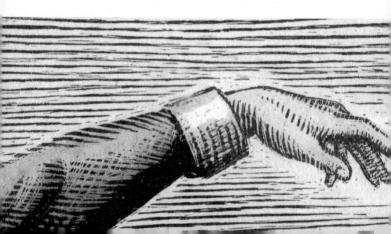

And the king was moved, and went up to the chamber over the gate, and wept: and as he went, thus he said, O my son Absalom, my son, my son Absalom: would God I had died for thee, O Absalom, my son, my son.

II SAMUEL 18:33

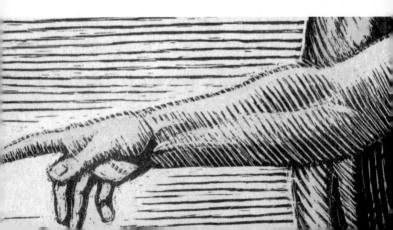

48. time

...learn to jest in good time; there's a time for
all things.

THE COMEDY OF ERRORS, ACT II, SCENE 2

*To all things there is an appointed time, and
a time to every purpose under the heaven....
A time to weep, and a time to laugh: a time to
mourn, and a time to dance.*

ECCLESIASTES 3:1, 4

Ben Jonson, one of Shakespeare's contemporaries who also was a poet and playwright, once said of Shakespeare that he "was not of an age, but for all time."

49. the high road

We must do good against evil.

ALL'S WELL THAT ENDS WELL, ACT II, SCENE 5

Be not overcome of evil, but overcome evil with goodness.

ROMANS 12:21

50. blessed quietness

Thy greatest helpe is quiet, gentle Nell:
I pray thee, sort thy heart to patience,...

KING HENRY VI PART II, ACT II, SCENE 4

*For thus said the Lord God, the Holy One of
Israel, In rest and quietness shall ye be saved: in
quietness and in confidence shall be your strength,
but ye would not.*

ISAIAH 30:15

51. evenhandedness

…death for death!
Haste still pays haste, and leisure answers
leisure;
Like doth quit like, and Measure still for
Measure.

MEASURE FOR MEASURE, ACT V, SCENE 1

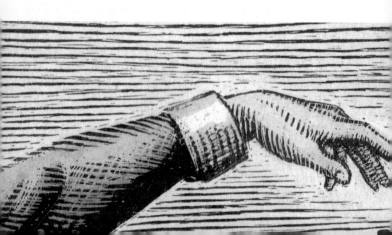

For with what judgment ye judge, ye shall be judged, and with what measure ye mete, it shall be measured to you again.

MATTHEW 7:2

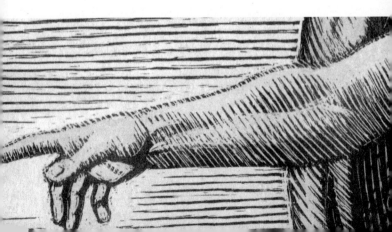

52. strength

Samson, master, he was a man of good carriage,
great carriage; for he carried the towngates on his
back like a porter, and he was in love.

LOVE'S LABOUR'S LOST, ACT I, SCENE 2

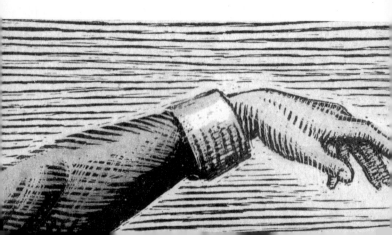

And Samson slept till midnight, and arose at midnight, and took the doors of the gates of the city, and the two posts and lifted them away with the bars, and put them upon his shoulders, and carried them up to the top of the mountain that is before Hebron.

JUDGES 16:3

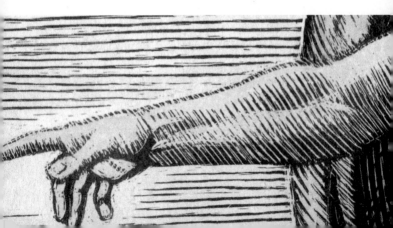

53. contentment

My Crowne is in my heart, not on my head:
Not deck'd with Diamonds and Indian stones:
Nor to be seene; my Crowne is call'd
    "Content,"
A crowne it is, that sildome Kings enjoy

KING HENRY VI PART III, ACT I, SCENE 3

But godliness is great gain, if a man be content
with that he hath. For we brought nothing into the
world, and it is certain, that we can carry nothing
out.

I TIMOTHY 6:6–7

William Shakespeare was buried in Holy Trinity Church, his parish church, in Stratford-upon-Avon. On his gravestone are these words:

Good friend, for Jesus' sake forbear
To dig the dust enclosed here.
Blest be the man that spares these stones,
And curst be he that moves my bones.

54. prudence

O my Antonio, I do know of these
That therefore only are reputed wise
For saying nothing; when I am very sure,
If they should speak, would almost damn
    those ears
Which, hearing them, would call their
    brothers fools.

THE MERCHANT OF VENICE, ACT I, SCENE 1

*Even a fool (when he holdeth his peace) is counted
wise, and he that stoppeth his lips, prudent.*

PROVERBS 17:28

55. addressing wrongdoings

> To revenge is no valour, but to bear.

TIMON OF ATHENS, ACT III, SCENE 5

Dearly beloved, avenge not yourselves, but give place unto wrath: for it is written, Vengeance is mine: I will repay, saith the Lord.

ROMANS 12:19

56. character

Yet eyes this cunning want to grace their art;
They draw but what they see, know not the
    heart.

SONNET 24

*But the Lord said unto Samuel, Look not on
his countenance, nor on the height of his stature,
because I have refused him: for God seeth not
as man seeth: for man looketh on the outward
appearance, but the Lord beholdeth the heart.*

I SAMUEL 16:7

57. boldness

Virtue is bold, and goodness never fearful.

MEASURE FOR MEASURE, ACT III, SCENE 1

The wicked flee when none pursueth: but the righteous are bold as a lion.

PROVERBS 28:1

58. faith-filled prayer

And my ending is despair,
Unless I be relieved by prayer,
Which pierces so that it assaults
Mercy itself, and frees all faults.

THE TEMPEST, EPILOGUE

Is any sick among you? Let him call for the Elders
of the Church, and let them pray for him, and
anoint him with oil in the Name of the Lord.
And the prayer of faith shall save the sick, and the
Lord shall raise him up: and if he have committed
sin, it shall be forgiven him.

JAMES 5:14–15

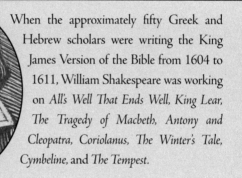

When the approximately fifty Greek and Hebrew scholars were writing the King James Version of the Bible from 1604 to 1611, William Shakespeare was working on *All's Well That Ends Well*, *King Lear*, *The Tragedy of Macbeth*, *Antony and Cleopatra*, *Coriolanus*, *The Winter's Tale*, *Cymbeline*, and *The Tempest*.

59. temperance

O God, that men should put an enemy in
   their mouths to steal away their brains!
   that we should with joy, pleasance, revel,
   pleasure and applause, transform ourselves
   into beasts!

OTHELLO, ACT II, SCENE 3

*Wine is a mocker and strong drink is raging: and
whosoever is deceived thereby, is not wise.*

PROVERBS 20:1

60. proper repairs

As patches, set upon a little breach, Discredit
more the hiding of the fault, Than did the
fault before it was so patched!

KING JOHN, ACT IV, SCENE 2

*Moreover no man pieceth an old garment with a
piece of new cloth: for that that should fill it up,
taketh away from the garment, and the breach is
worse.*

MATTHEW 9:16

61. purposeful pain

Sweet are the uses of adversity,
Which like the toad, ugly and venomous,
Wears yet a precious jewel in his head;

AS YOU LIKE IT, ACT II, SCENE 1

It is good for me that I have been afflicted, that I
may learn thy statutes.

PSALM 119:71

62. reputation

Who steals my purse, steals trash…
But he that filches from me my good name
Robs me of that which not enriches him
And makes me poor indeed.

OTHELLO, ACT III, SCENE 3

A good name is to be chosen above great riches,
and loving favor is above silver and above gold.

PROVERBS 22:1

63. true friendship

A friend should bear his friend's infirmities,
But Brutus makes mine greater than they are.

THE TRAGEDY OF JULIUS CAESAR, ACT IV, SCENE 3

We which are strong, ought to bear the infirmities
of the weak, and not to please ourselves.

ROMANS 15:1

64. divine providence

Our indiscretion sometimes serves us well
When our deep plots do pall; and that should
    learn us
There's a divinity that shapes our ends,
Rough-hew them how we will—

HAMLET, PRINCE OF DENMARK, ACT V, SCENE 2

The king's heart is in the hand of the Lord, as the rivers of waters: he turneth it whithersoever it pleaseth him.

PROVERBS 21:1

The beginnings of the Bible in the English language started with John Wycliffe. He began to espouse that Scripture—not monarchs or religious leaders—was the prime authority for truth and justice. Between 1380 and 1400, he translated the first complete Bible in the English language from the Latin Vulgate.

65. moderation

Let's teach ourselves that honourable stop,
Not to outsport discretion.

OTHELLO, ACT II, SCENE 3

Let your patient mind be known unto all men.
The Lord is at hand.

PHILIPPIANS 4:5

66. humility

Pride is his own glass, his own trumpet,
his own chronicle; and whatever praises itself
but in the deed, devours the deed in the praise.

TROILUS AND CRESSIDA, ACT I, SCENE 3

Let another man praise thee, and not thine own
mouth: a stranger, and not thine own lips.

PROVERBS 27:2

67. confidentiality

Thou shalt never get such a secret from me
    but by a parable.

THE TWO GENTLEMEN OF VERONA, ACT II, SCENE 5

*Then the disciples came, and said to him, Why
speakest thou to them in parables? And he
answered and said unto them, Because it is given
unto you, to know the secrets of the kingdom of
heaven, but to them it is not given.*

MATTHEW 13:10–11

68. compassion

A widow cries;
Be husband to me, heavens!

KING JOHN, ACT III, SCENE 1

*For he that made thee, is thine husband (whose
name is the Lord of hosts) and thy Redeemer the
Holy One of Israel, shall be called the God of the
whole world.*

ISAIAH 54:5

69. just leaders

He who the sword of heaven will bear
Should be as holy as severe.

MEASURE FOR MEASURE, ACT III, SCENE 2

The God of Israel spake to me, the strength of Israel said, Thou shalt bear rule over men, being just, and ruling in the fear of God.

II SAMUEL 23:3

70. mercy

How shalt thou hope for mercy, rendering
    none?
…For as thou urgest justice, be assur'd
Thou shalt have justice, more than thou
    desir'st.

THE MERCHANT OF VENICE, ACT IV, SCENE 1

For there shall be judgment merciless to him that showeth no mercy, and mercy rejoiceth against judgment.

JAMES 2:13

71. justice

So just is God, to right the innocent.

KING RICHARD III, ACT I, SCENE 3

*For the Lord loveth judgment, and forsaketh not
his saints: they shall be preserved forevermore: but
the seed of the wicked shall be cut off.*

PSALM 37:28

72. self-sufficiency

Neither a borrower nor a lender be:
For loan oft loses both itself and friend;

HAMLET, PRINCE OF DENMARK, ACT I, SCENE 3

The rich ruleth the poor, and the borrower is servant to the man that lendeth.

PROVERBS 22:7

73. marriage

God, the best maker of all marriages,
Combine your hearts in one....

KING HENRY V, ACT V, SCENE 2

*Therefore shall man leave his father and his
mother, and shall cleave to his wife, and they shall
be one flesh.*

GENESIS 2:24

74. caution

Give every man thine ear, but few thy voice:

HAMLET, PRINCE OF DENMARK, ACT I, SCENE 3

Wherefore my dear brethren, let every man be swift to hear, slow to speak, and slow to wrath.

JAMES 1:19

75. restoration

How can I then return in happy plight
That am debarr'd the benefit of rest?
When day's oppression is not eased by night,
But day by night, and night by day oppressed.

SONNET 28

*Come unto me, all ye that are weary and laden,
and I will ease you. Take my yoke on you, and
learn of me, that I am meek and lowly in heart:
and ye shall find rest unto your souls.*

MATTHEW 11:28–29

76. forgiveness

I as free forgive you
As I would be forgiven.

KING HENRY VIII, ACT II, SCENE 1

*And forgive us our sins: for even we forgive every
man that is indebted to us: And lead us not into
temptation: but deliver us from evil.*

MATTHEW 6:12–13

77. peacemakers

For blessed are the Peace-makers on Earth.

KING HENRY VI PART II, ACT II, SCENE 1

Blessed are the peacemakers: for they shall be called the children of God.

MATTHEW 5:9

78. trustworthiness

There's no trust,
No faith, no honesty in men: all perjur'd,
All forsworn, all naught, all dissemblers.

THE TRAGEDY OF ROMEO AND JULIET, ACT III, SCENE 2

*Put not your trust in princes, nor in the son of man,
for there is none help in him. His breath departeth,
and he returneth to his earth: then his thoughts
perish. Blessed is he, that hath the God of Jacob for
his help, whose hope is in the Lord his God. Which
made heaven and earth, the sea, and all that therein
is: which keepeth his fidelity forever.*

PSALM 146:3–5

79. holy matrimony

No, God forbid that I should wish them
   sever'd
Whom God hath joind together.

KING HENRY VI PART III, ACT IV, SCENE 1

Wherefore they are no more twain, but one flesh.
Let not man therefore put asunder that, which
God hath coupled together.

MATTHEW 19:6

80. Christian unity

Hath not a Jew eyes? hath not a Jew hands, organs,
dementions, sences, affections, passions, fed with
the same foode, hurt with the same weapons,
subject to the same diseases, healed by the same
meanes, warmed and cooled by the same Winter
and Sommer as a Christian is?

THE MERCHANT OF VENICE, ACT III, SCENE 1

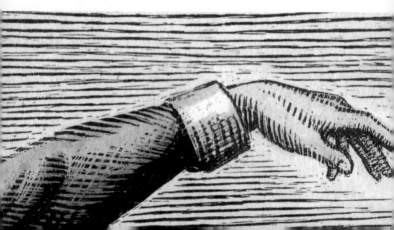

There is neither Jew nor Grecian: there is neither bond nor free: there is neither male nor female: for ye are all one in Christ Jesus.

GALATIANS 3:28

Shakespeare's England suffered from racial and other kinds of prejudices. Jews, people of color, and others who were considered different met discrimination. Shakespeare's plays reflected his culture, yet his characters, such as Othello and Shylock, are complex characters who invite readers to know them beyond ethnicity and race.

81. primacy of God

'Tis mad idolatry
To make the service greater than the god…

TROILUS AND CRESSIDA, ACT II, SCENE 2

Having a show of godliness, but have denied the power thereof: turn away therefore from such.

II TIMOTHY 3:5

82. love, the highest law

For charity itself fulfils the law.

LOVE'S LABOUR'S LOST, ACT IV, SCENE 3

Love doeth not evil to his neighbor: therefore is love the fulfilling of the Law.

ROMANS 13:10

83. unending praise

Let never Day nor Night unhallow'd passe,
But still remember what the Lord hath done.

KING HENRY VI PART II, ACT II, SCENE 1

The Lord's name is praised from the rising of the
sun, unto the going down of the same.

PSALM 113:3

84. love everlasting

…love is not love
Which alters when it alteration finds,
Or bends with the remover to remove.
O no, it is an ever-fixed mark
That looks on tempests and is never shaken;…
Love alters not with his brief hours and weeks,
But bears it out even to the edge of doom:

SONNET 116

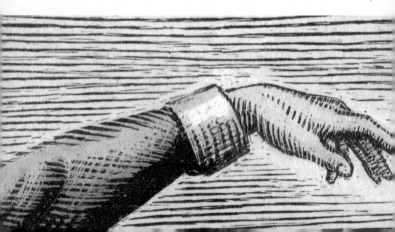

It suffereth all things: it believeth all things: it hopeth all things: it endureth all things. Love doth never fall away....

I CORINTHIANS 13:7–8

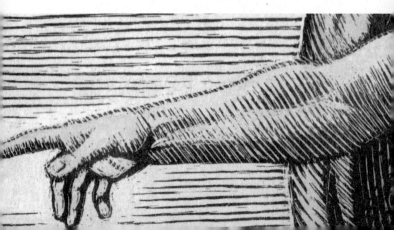

85. God's creation

...all is in His hands above.

THE MERRY WIVES OF WINDSOR, ACT I, SCENE 4

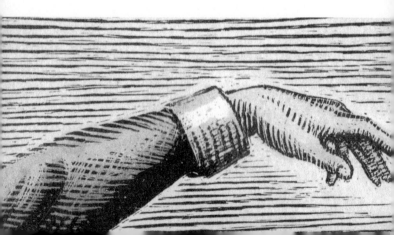

In whose hand are the deep places of the earth, and the heights of the mountains are his: To whom the sea belongeth: for he made it, and his hands formed the dry land. Come, let us worship and fall down, and kneel before the Lord our maker.

PSALM 95:4–6

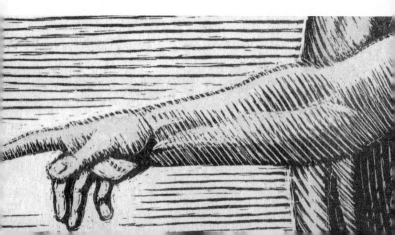

86. the gift of life

O Lord, that lends me life,
Lend me a heart repleate with thankfulnesse:

KING HENRY VI PART II, ACT I, SCENE 1

Thou hast given me life, and grace: and thy visitation hath preserved my spirit.

JOB 10:12

William Shakespeare's birth date can't be confirmed with 100 percent accuracy, but church records show that he was baptized on April 26, 1564. Most biographers believe he was born on April 23, which, coincidentally, is the date of his death in 1616.

87. the certainty of death

By med'cine life may be prolong'd, yet death
Will seize the doctor too.

CYMBELINE, ACT V, SCENE 5

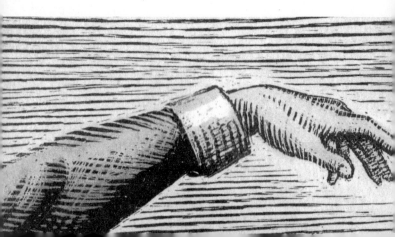

What man liveth, and shall not see death? Shall he deliver his soul from the hand of the grave? Selah.

PSALM 89:48

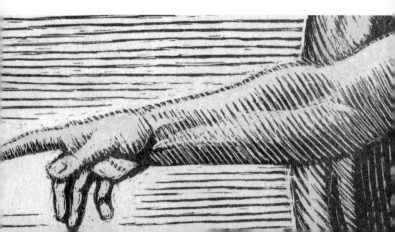

88. unimaginable goodness

The eye of man hath not heard, the ear of man hath
not seen, man's hand is not able to taste, his tongue to
conceive, nor his heart to report what my dream was.

A MIDSUMMER NIGHT'S DREAM, ACT IV, SCENE 1

*But as it is written, The things which eye hath not
seen, neither ear hath heard, neither came into
man's heart, are, which God hath prepared for
them that love him. But God hath revealed them
unto us by his Spirit: for the Spirit searcheth all
things, yea, the deep things of God.*

I CORINTHIANS 2:9–10

89. glorifying God

Praise be God, and not our strength for it:

KING HENRY V, ACT IV, SCENE 7

Not unto us, O Lord, not unto us, but unto thy
Name give the glory, for thy loving mercy and for
thy truth's sake.

PSALM 115:1

90. God, our creator

The King of Kings, the glorious God of heaven,
Who in six daies did frame his heavenly worke,
And made all things to stand in perfect course.
Then to his image he did make a man,
Old Adam, and, from his side asleepe,
A rib was taken, of which the Lord did make,
The woe of man so term'd by Adam then....

TAMING OF THE SHREW, ACT V, SCENE 2

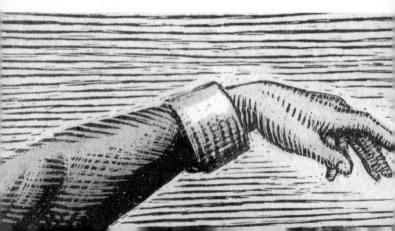

In the beginning God created the heaven and the earth.... Thus God created the man in his image: in the image of God created he him: he created them male and female.

GENESIS 1:1, 27

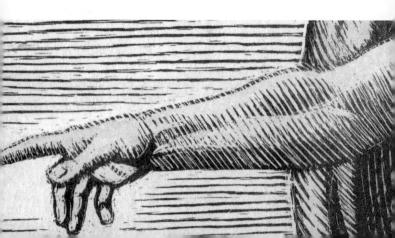

91. the essence of love

Feed where thou wilt, on mountain or in dale:
Graze on my lips, and if those hills be dry,
Stray lower, where the pleasant fountains lie.

VENUS AND ADONIS

*Arise, O north, and come O south, and blow on
my garden that the spices thereof may flow out: let
my well beloved come to his garden, and eat his
pleasant fruit.*

SONG OF SOLOMON 4:16

92. immeasurable love

Ile set a bourne how farre to be belov'd.

THE TRAGEDY OF ANTONY AND
CLEOPATRA, ACT I, SCENE 1

*That Christ may dwell in your hearts by faith,
that ye, being rooted and grounded in love, May
be able to comprehend with all Saints, what is
the breadth, and length, and depth, and height:
And to know the love of Christ, which passeth
knowledge, that ye may be filled with all fullness
of God.*

EPHESIANS 3:17–19

93. eternal perspective

When to the sessions of sweet silent thought,
I summon up remembrance of things past,
I sigh the lack of many a thing I sought,
And with old woes new wail my dear time's
    waste:

SONNET 30

*Teach us so to number our days, that we may
apply our hearts unto wisdom.*

PSALM 90:12

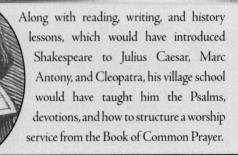

Along with reading, writing, and history lessons, which would have introduced Shakespeare to Julius Caesar, Marc Antony, and Cleopatra, his village school would have taught him the Psalms, devotions, and how to structure a worship service from the Book of Common Prayer.

94. God, our victor

O God, thy Arme was here:
And not to us, but to thy Arme along,
Ascribe we all:…take it, God
For it is none but thine.

KING HENRY V, ACT IV, SCENE 8

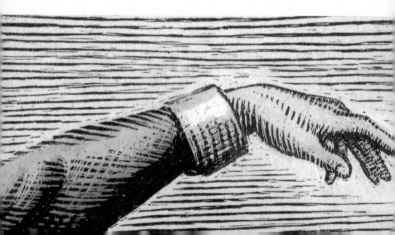

Sing unto the Lord a new song: for he hath done marvelous things: his right hand, and his holy arm have gotten him the victory.

PSALM 98:1

95. God's workmanship

What a piece of work is man! How noble in reason! How infinite in faculties! In form, in moving, how express and admirable! In action, how like an angel! In apprehension, how like a god! The beauty of the world! The paragon of animals! And yet, to me, what is this quintessence of dust?

HAMLET, PRINCE OF DENMARK, ACT II, SCENE 2

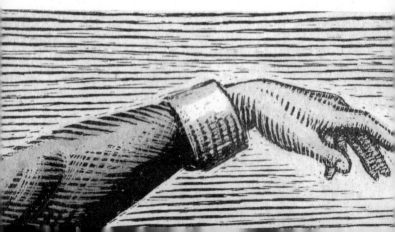

What is man, say I, that thou art mindful of him?
And the son of man, that thou visitest him? For
thou hast made him a little lower than God, and
crowned him with glory and worship. Thou hast
made him to have dominion in the works of thine
hands, thou hast put all things under his feet.

PSALM 8:4–6

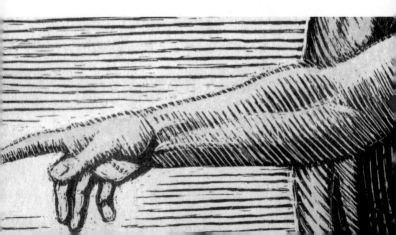

96. Christ, our redeemer

…those holy fields
Over whose acres walk'd those blessed feet
Which fourteen hundred years ago were nail'd
For our advantage on the bitter cross.

KING HENRY IV PART I, ACT I, SCENE 1

*How beautiful upon the mountains are the feet
of him, that declareth and publisheth peace? That
declareth good tidings, and publisheth salvation,
saying unto Zion, Thy God reigneth?*

ISAIAH 52:7

97. God's Word, our guide

And God shall be my hope, my stay, my guide,
And Lanthorne to my feete.

KING HENRY VI PART II, ACT II, SCENE 3

*Thy word is a lantern unto my feet, and a light
unto my path.*

PSALM 119:105

When he was a young child, Shakespeare's school would have given him a hornbook, which was a wooden paddle that had a sheet of parchment pasted to it. Written on the parchment were the English alphabet and a religious prayer.

98. godly wisdom

Not from the stars do I my judgement pluck,
And yet methinks I have astronomy,
But not to tell of good, or evil luck,
Of plagues, of dearths, or season's quality...
  But from thine eyes my knowledge I derive.

SONNET 14

If any of you lack wisdom, let him ask of God,
that giveth to all men liberally, and upbraideth
not; and it shall be given him.

JAMES 1:5

99. unconditional love

Love sought is good, but given unsought is
   better.

TWELFTH NIGHT, ACT III, SCENE 1

*But God setteth out his love toward us, seeing that
while we were yet sinners, Christ died for us.*

ROMANS 5:8

Although Shakespeare's personal faith is uncertain, based on the number of references to Scripture and biblical images in his works, it's quite likely that he grew up reading and listening to Scripture.

100. eternal love

In life thou lived'st, in death thou died'st
    beloved.

FUNERAL ELEGY

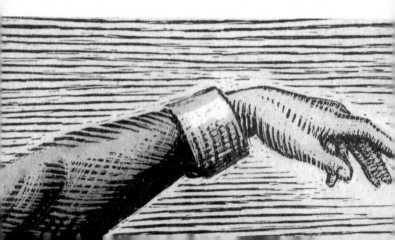

Then I heard a voice from heaven, saying unto me, Write, Blessed are the dead, which hereafter die in the Lord. Even so saith the Spirit: for they rest from their labors, and their works follow them.

REVELATION 14:13

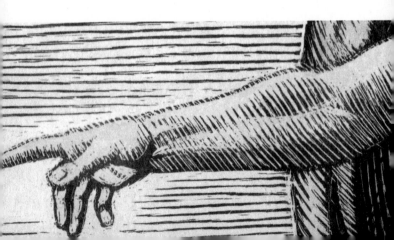

101. life's purpose

…we are borne to do benefits.

THE LIFE OF TIMON OF ATHENS, ACT 1, SCENE 2

For we are his workmanship created in Christ Jesus unto good works, which God hath ordained, that we should walk in them.

EPHESIANS 2:10

BIBLIOGRAPHY

Baker, Christopher. *Shakespeare in an Hour*. Hanover, New Hampshire: In an Hour Books, 2009.

Bragg, Melvyn. *The Book of Books: The Radical Impact of the King James Bible 1611–2011*. Berkeley: Counterpoint, 2011.

Doyle, John. *Shakespeare for Dummies*. Foster City, Calif: IDG Books Worldwide, 1999.

Fox, Levi. *The Shakespeare Handbook: The Essential Companion to Shakespeare's Works, Life and Times*. Boston: G. K. Hall & Co, 1987.

Eaton, Thomas Ray. *Shakespeare and the Bible*. New York: AMS Press, 1972.

Hamlin, Hannibal. "Shakespeare and the King James Bible: Ships Passing in the Night." Manifold Greatness Blog. N.p., 29 Nov. 2011. Web. 22 Mar. 2016.

Jeffcoat, John. "English Bible History: Timeline of How We Got the English Bible." N.p., n.d. Web. 22 Mar. 2016.

LeMonico, Michael. *Shakespeare 101*. New York: Gramercy Books, Random House, 2001.

Mabillard, Amanda. "Metaphors in Shakespeare's Macbeth—A Detailed Look at Biblical Imagery in the Tragedy Macbeth." N.p., n.d. Web. 22 Mar. 2016.